PRAYERS

—— OF THE ——

RIGHTEOUS

ARLINDA MCGEE

ISBN 979-8-88644-561-9 (Paperback)
ISBN 979-8-88644-562-6 (Digital)

Copyright © 2023 Arlinda McGee
All rights reserved
First Edition

All rights reserved. No part of this publication may be reproduced, distributed, or transmitted in any form or by any means, including photocopying, recording, or other electronic or mechanical methods without the prior written permission of the publisher. For permission requests, solicit the publisher via the address below.

Covenant Books
11661 Hwy 707
Murrells Inlet, SC 29576
www.covenantbooks.com

DISCLAIMER

Throughout this book, I will use Hebrew versions of God's name. *Elohim* is defined as the only creator of the universe. Although it is the Hebrew meaning of *God* or *gods*, I am referring to a single deity in masculine form, the God of Israel. I will use *heavenly Father, the Most High, Yah, or Yahuah* interchangeably with *Elohim (Elohiym)* rather than using *Lord* or *God*.

I will also reference the Hebrew term *Yahshua HaMashiach* or the *Messiah* instead of Jesus Christ or Yeshua, widely expressed English terms. Ruach Ha-Kodesh will be used rather than the Holy Spirit.

The use of these names is a personal preference and is not intended to offend or confuse anyone. If you prefer to say or think the English-name versions of God and Jesus, it is totally up to you. My intent is to share spiritual experiences and get the message of prayer across to the audience. Testimonies of others will obtain "God," "Lord," and "Jesus" because it is what they quoted. I will also use the English-translated names in my own testimonies if it was in a time frame I said it.

I am not affiliated with extremist religious groups or persons of any kind. I consider myself a set-apart individual who desires to share testimonies and stories for purposes of spiritual validation, growth, and enhancement.

INTRODUCTION

If today was my last day to live, it would be the perfect time to humble my heart. I would pray for forgiveness, take responsibility for my wrongs, and try to present the best version of myself within the limited space and time I have left. There would be no room for disparities, and my focus would be gratefulness for every breath inhaled and exhaled. When I am not full of myself or drowned by the cares of this world, this is a mindset I try to remember in prayer time.

Prayer is my assurance and way of escape regardless of the highs and lows of life. In dire times, I have made requests known to the heavenly Father and waited for His divine intervention. Even while working on this book project, I've grieved the death of a grandchild who was delivered stillborn. Great emotions of sadness led to agony; however, I am yet praying.

How can I make prayer my source after this hurtful reality? Through relationship with the Most High, I fully trust Him even when things are incomprehensible to human intellect and seem unfair. I believe things happen for a greater purpose, so I continue to pray while there is breath in my body.

It is my testimony that victories and milestones were birthed in my life through prayer. It has become the centerpiece of my life and brought forth permanent change. No matter the trial, tribulation, or temptation in life, I am a witness that prayer works through faith.

Through experience, I've learned that when opening up to Elohim, His involvement in our lives is precise. Regardless of what is going on in the world or the curve balls of life, prayer offers real solutions. Praying and asking to discern between good and evil invite justice and help us walk in righteousness, which is the core purpose of this book.

The most important factor of prayer is who we are praying to, the condition of the heart when praying, and sincere belief. Understanding the purpose of prayer and exercising its function are foundational and give life a whole new meaning. By sharing some of my own personal testimonies and the testimonies of others, I hope you will learn, relate, experience, or maintain an intimate prayer connection of your own.

PART 1

PERSONAL PRAYER EXPERIENCES

Chapter 1

An Unforgettable Prayer Encounter

It was the year 1998, and I was on my knees around 4:00 a.m. In much anguish, I cried out, "Lord, help me please!" Repeatedly, I said, "Please, Lord, I need you."

Tightly gripping on the thin white-quilted blanket tossed across the bed, I begin to lift my voice. "I am tired. I am so tired."

Unbroken tears from my red puffy eyes rushed down my cheekbones while my lips quivered at the same time. In between a couple sniffles, I attempted to get the words out of my mouth. Intense emotions caused my words to be broken. I could feel my body temperature slightly rising and sweat beading on my forehead as anxiety increased.

Lifting up my bowed-down head and gazing toward the ceiling in my dark bedroom that reflected a dim red light from my digital clock, I sobbed, "I can't take it no more."

No one else was around except my two sons snoozing in their bunk beds and my baby girl sound asleep in her crib in the adjacent room eight feet away. To my surprise, the whimpering and crying did not wake them up. What a sleepless night!

Hours of tossing and turning and what seemed like a never-ending wrestling match with the blanket left me restless. The agony within was so massive. Shifting my body from my knees to a quick flop on the unpolished hardwood floor, I began rocking back and forth. Thank goodness I was alone because someone would have thought that I was a crazy lady.

No longer crying out and in a whispered tone, I said, "Father, I can't live like this anymore. I want you in my life."

Besides being physically and emotionally exhausted, my soul was tattered and torn. The internal pain pierced deep enough to keep my attention suspended in this moment.

The storms of life were finally taking a toll. So many twists and turns had taken place in my life, and I was only twenty-five years old. In my quest to feel loved and accepted, here I sat feeling abandoned, overwhelmed, worthless, scorned, and brokenhearted. A multiplicity of life stressors seemed to follow me everywhere. Besides failing relationships, here I was in the late nineties having already moved to three different states with children.

We moved back and forth to Kansas City from a rural area in California, a small town in Mississippi, and the outskirts of Denver, Colorado. It was obvious that the itch for adventure, the new scenery, and chasing opportunities from city to city did not fill my void. I still landed back in Kansas City.

My return to Kansas City opened doors for me to become a young homeowner with two paid-off cars in the driveway and a twice-promoted employee of a growing company while in pursuit to become an entrepreneur at the same time. I was doing okay as a young single mother with three children at the time.

Opening up to the heavenly Father seemed to be my final option for answers, and I needed relief from inner turmoil and strife, relationship obsessions, a false sense of success, and other life failures. I knew I was missing something more meaningful. *There must be more to life than this*, I thought. Because I felt so helpless, I cried out in distress. In my heart, I wanted solutions, and my soul desired direction.

During this unforgettable prayer event, the Most High confronted me about forgiveness. My instant thought was, *Forgive who?* My other thought was, *Why now?* I could not believe that this suggestion was interrupting my sobbing moment. It did not seem to fit my woes, but there was a strong internal sense and feeling that I was to forgive.

I knew I was being directed supernaturally. What was happening was too powerful to ignore. I just knew that it was my stepfather, James, that I needed to forgive. From the age of eleven years old, I despised him. There was not a person or situation that could top the hatred in my heart against him.

The horrific memory of being raped by a stranger near a city bus stop at age fifteen did not compare to the level of disgust I had toward this man. He never abused or violated me personally. I just always felt that he was sent from hell to disrupt our family harmony.

My mother was a jewel to the seven children she had at the time James entered our lives in the early eighties. She was a role model to me. Growing up, I completely admired her. She was mostly soft-spoken, fun, intelligent, modestly dressed, a teacher to all of us, and a woman of her word. She loved the heavenly Father.

She was overall graceful to look at and be around. Mom spent precious moments talking to us about morals and values. She went out of her way to make not just me but all her children feel special.

The seed of anger was planted the morning I walked down the stairs of my childhood home. Shockingly, this man who I thought was an intruder was laying on our living room sofa snoring loudly.

I yelled, "Who is that?"

Rushing back up the stairs to my mother's bedroom, I said, "Mama, who is that big Black man snoring on our couch?"

She gave no explanation. She said, "Go on to school, and I will explain later."

Well, later turned into two long weeks. We stared at him, and he did not speak a mumbling word to us the whole time, not even a hello. The nerve of this man! My siblings and I huddled in growing suspicion of who this stranger was the first few days. One of my brothers figured he was there to help our mother out with all of us, and we accepted that he had Mom's permission to be there.

At this point, we assumed that he was like her boyfriend. Nevertheless, that did not take away the feeling of violation. A small seed of anger was planted in me the first day and festered thereafter.

No man had ever lived with us before, so I kept thinking, *Why is he here?* I would peek around the corner of the wall near the stairwell hoping he would get up from the couch and walk out the door forever.

Finally, at the end of two weeks, my mother sat us all down and had a family discussion. This was a routine she did with us to correct misbehavior, to communicate household rules, to inform of upcoming events and changes, and for planning purposes. Of course, this roundtable discussion was about James living with us. I was devastated because he came out of nowhere and was now part of our family.

I felt like James robbed my mother's joy when he dominated the atmosphere with drunkenness off and on for years. When he was sober, he catered to my mother like a queen. The love in my mother's eyes for him during his sobriety made life tolerable with him around. It was comforting to see her happy.

However, when James was intoxicated, his behavior was drastically altered. He was very loud, careless, and super talkative. It was annoying to watch how the aftereffects of alcohol ended with some sort of chaos and commotion inside or outside the house. The sad countenance my mother wore when James was drinking was a heavy burden to behold.

The only two things that did not make me prejudice was James' cooking and my little sister he and my mom had together. She was the eighth child. Other than that, it was satisfying to roll my eyes at him, turn up my nose, and make some kind of ill remark every chance I could. As a result of my mother's decision to stay with him and marry him, I allowed unforgiveness to take residence.

The prayer encounter I had with Elohim disclosed the rooted bitterness against James. Brokenness led to confrontation, and this single event invited me into a whole new world of spiritual communication. The dialogue between me and the heavenly Father filtered through my conscience and was the beginning of my individual prayer language.

According to Baesler (2012), "Like learning to speak and building one's vocabulary, the communicative nature of prayer grows and changes in accordance with development and context in one's life." My damaged emotions fueled by unforgiveness and bitterness built up for years and was unrighteous. When my heart was in a state of tenderness, conviction came. Prayer emerged, and it changed the course of my life.

CHAPTER 2

Confess your faults one to another,
and pray for one another, that ye may be healed.
The effectual fervent prayer of the righteous man
avails much.

—James 5:16 (Cepher Bible)

Prayer Exposed My Heart

My private prayer encounter with the Most High exposed what had to be removed from the seat of my soul. In this world, it is not uncommon for people to make decisions to appease their personal interest.

For instance, it was my mom's choice to love James. Despite her decision and the effect it had on me, I was responsible for my own poisoned thoughts against my stepfather. Mom had to live with her decision to be with him, and I was charged with my response to her choice.

As the Father above began exposing the condition of my heart the day I sincerely cried out for His help, I was reminded of Mark 11:25, which says, "And whenever you stand praying, forgive, if you have anything against anyone, so that your Father also who is in heaven may forgive you your trespasses."

Before entering a new journey, spiritual heart surgery had to take place. Prayer enlightened me that forgiveness was the foundation I needed to move forward toward healing and freedom.

Prayer comes with a set of instructions too. I will never forget the moment I picked up the phone to call James immediately after my prayer encounter. It was shortly before 5:00 a.m. This call was fourteen years after the first time I ever laid eyes on him.

After being exposed to my shortcomings, I was embarrassed to call, but I had to. I was remorseful and wanted to apologize to him. This feeling was so strong and knowable that it is hard to describe. James was under the impression that I already forgave him because of the bond he built with my first son. I still secretly hated him.

For my son's sake, I allowed their relationship as grandfather and grandson to flourish and concealed my feelings against him. I saw it as sacrificing for my son, but the anger and bitterness still put my eternal soul at risk. Now I was faced with revealing where I really stood. Deception and truth cannot abide together, so it was time to fess up.

I picked up the phone slowly and couldn't believe I was actually dialing his number. James picked up the phone after the second ring.

He said, "Hello."

I said, "Hi, James, good morning."

I could tell he was drinking throughout the night, but he was not fully intoxicated.

"Your mother is asleep," he said.

I said, "Well, I called for you."

"What's wrong? What happened?" he said.

With the phone resting between my shoulder and jawbone, I said, "I owe you an apology."

I apologized for all the times I disrespected him and began sharing my dark thoughts against him. Our conversation lasted about two hours. I got used to disliking him, and I never even recall having a ten-minute civil conversation with him. On this day, I was freed from the bondage of resentment, rebellion, and unforgiveness.

Once I asked for his forgiveness, a weight was lifted from me. Positive thoughts about James started rushing in, and I saw him in a different light as darkness was removed from me. On this day of prayer, I was restored.

Getting rid of malice in one's heart is needed for the heavenly Father to blot out our transgressions. One of the reasons it is so important to always pray is to function in life with a clean heart. A scripture I frequently recite is, "Create in me a clean heart O' Yah and renew a right spirit within me."

When disappointment festers, the hurt we feel takes root within and summons negativity and criticism toward others. Bitterness kills the soul. Unforgiveness, regardless of the offence, can poison every area of a person's life.

Ephesians 4:31–32 (Cepher Bible) command, "Let all bitterness, and wrath, and anger, and clamor, and evil speaking be put away from you, with all malice: and be ye kind one to another, tenderhearted, forgiving one another even as Elohiym for Mashiach's sake has forgiven you."

When someone else is suffering from unforgiveness, I can spot it. Not long ago, I shared this particular testimony with a couple teenagers. I explained how prayer delivered me from anger and bitterness. Unclean spirits had a grip on me for years and affected my heart and insight.

I talked with them about how I was accountable for choosing to have hate toward my stepfather. This could be easily measured by six other siblings in the same household who also did not like what was going on with my stepfather, but they did not hate him. The issue was within me.

It was not the first time I spoke to the teenagers about praying through circumstances. On other occasions, they told me how "that prayer thing" worked for them. Their recent concern was almost identical to my stepfather, James, and I. Since I could relate to their feelings that others disregarded, I had their full attention.

They confided in me and were opened to hear any solution. We spent hours discussing how hostility interferes with forgiveness and how prolonged reactions intertwine with personality. I did not want them to agonize within like I once did. After explaining how forgiveness works and its continuous process, prayer was the antidote.

This time, I told the teenagers that I would pray earnestly on their behalf with understanding that we would all pray about the situation. My heart went out to them, and I did not want them to be crippled in life by resentment.

I told them to expect change no matter how it was distributed. Although the circumstance did not change in their household right away, the result of prayer eventually brought a favorable and peaceful outcome. Oh, what joy prayer brings.

Harboring ill feelings against someone is spiritual suicide. It is torment and contamination to all kinds of relationships. I cannot express this enough. After living with this ugly nature for a long time, I purposed in my heart not to ever go back. Since I once lived it, I try to help others through it or go in secret warfare on their behalf during private prayer time.

I am so glad that this personal revival took place before James' death. Temptation to resent him again popped up every now and then, but it did not stick. It could not because I was truly delivered and did not want to be shackled.

—

CHAPTER 3

*Call unto me and I will answer you
and show you great and mighty things,
which you know not.*
—Jeremiah 33:3 (Cepher Bible)

Prayer Reveals

The one person you must lift up in prayer all your life is you. Spiritual development will come from praying for yourself. It is amazing how thousands of thoughts and hundreds of distractions a day dominate our senses and cloud our judgment. As a matter of fact, external things have so much influence; it can redefine and recondition who you really are.

Therefore, prayer must be a priority. The age of deception ran a number on so many people, and the worst kind is self-deception. It redirects knowledge of your true self. I remember praying, "Father, show me myself," and to my surprise, so much was revealed.

Prayer unfolded things about me, and when honestly analyzing events of life, I could vividly see where I took a wrong or right turn. The Holy Spirit (Ruach Ha-Kodesh) assists with bringing all things to our remembrance, and when taking a step back, we can categorize behavior under obedience or disobedience. There is no gray area. This is absolute in my opinion when it's all said and done.

When self-examination is pursued, it bypasses victimization and shows a reflection of the heart. We are without excuse for conducting ourselves poorly or immorally. Proverbs 14:10 even speaks on the heart knowing its own bitterness. There is always an opportunity to be better and chose what is right.

Why do people go the opposite direction when given instruction to do the right thing? When we are self-dependent and act on our own will without Elohim's help, it is easy to waiver. No one will reach a dead end without being warned first. We will all have to account for our individual motives and deeds.

The warning may come from parents, a family member, teacher, mentor, friends, a stranger, or a small still voice. Ultimately, we still chose our own path. It is simple for people to flee the presence of Elohim for self-serving reasons or to elude discipline, and ego will always fight to lead the way. However, choosing our way does not come without consequences. Isaiah 55:8 says, "For my thoughts are not your thoughts, neither are your ways my ways says Yahuah."

I spent years imagining how my life should go and what it should look like. I found out deception blinds the heart. I got used to giving first place to emotions, which led to distorted and unhealthy thoughts. The enemy's trickery is an ancient tactic used to lure people away from the right destiny, and sometimes, mind-altering events and trauma play a part as well.

When I inquired in prayer to see myself, I was shown that as a child, I wanted my parents in the same household. I was reminded of this impossibility as I frequently visited my father who remarried and had a daughter the exact same age as myself. We are only three months apart in age. I saw a family setup of man, woman, and child and could not understand why that was not the case at home with my mom and siblings.

When Mom remarried, maybe I would have grown to accept the structure if my stepdad was not an alcoholic. Who knows, I probably would have made some other excuse though. My whole childhood, I longed to be in the same household with my father.

He was active in my life and did an excellent job communicating with the four children he and my mother bore together but was not present full-time. I was the fourth child of their marriage, and they divorced later after I was born. I wanted the family in my adulthood the way I felt it should have been with my parents.

Historically, there is a rich heritage of a husband and father being the head of the household. Today, many households are fragmented, and there are many factors to consider for this dismantlement. We have entered an era of blended families being a societal norm.

Many of my decisions were subconsciously affected by this desire to have a picture-perfect family I held inside. I was so preoccupied with serving a certain image of family and felt the need to have a man around the house at any cost. I am still recovering from my decisions. In other words, I made unrealistic choices, which invited unnecessary trials and tribulations.

My life was spent trying to fix a broken home. If we are not careful, our own images and ideas can become gods. Meditating on my life cycles, I saw how I discarded and replaced people, not only to serve an image but also to attempt resolving an inner void on my own strength.

Prayer revealed how I entertained a deceptive message. I got played. It is the enemy's goal to entrap us at a young age by trauma and fear. Later in life, we figure out why certain things from childhood disrupted our peace in adulthood. Thankfully, prayer exposes false messages and opens us up for healing.

We are creative beings, and becoming someone you were not purposed to be can result in malfunctions and dysfunctions later in life that were never intended. It was never meant for me to elevate an image of any kind above the Creator. That is idolatry. Your pattern of life tells the real story of who or what you are really serving.

Life has a way of bringing someone to the end of themselves and their own agenda to fix attention back on Elohim. These life alignments come to bring everything back to its rightful perspective. It's a balancing act. Prayer is the tool to reassemble our lives. When I prayed, I was raw and transparent, and besides, I lied to myself long enough.

At my wit's end, I did not have time to speak eloquent words when praying, "Who am I, and what do you want from me?" The illusion of what I deemed a good life was discontinued. I overcame and pressed through trials, but there is a difference between small victories and life-changing moments.

Prayer opened my eyes to see where I really stood in life. It was like putting on spiritual goggles. I could see things clearer. Prayer will allow you to see your own faults and lead to repentance without blaming anyone else. The bottom line is, I saw how I took matters in my own hands.

Prayer will unfold the hidden things and openly manifest your purpose and path. This does not come without obstacles or copycat versions of who you are. It is imperative to incorporate prayer in your daily life to experience the essence of being in existence as "you" formed by the Creator.

For so long, I spent years observing and practicing traditions and cultures that shaped me. I worked tirelessly to become the person that lives by the standards others laid out for me without self-discovery. My existence was molded to please others. Whenever I got quiet within myself, I would say, "There must be more to me than going to church, having a family, being a consumer, having an enjoyable time, working a job or two, and keeping people happy."

We get so caught up in obtaining things and living a misguided version of ourselves that we miss the mark. After praying sometimes, I would hear, "Everything you need is inside of you." Everything in me connects back to the Creator Himself. To see Him and to know Him is to know thyself. Prayer can assist with knowing and maintaining your quest in life. To be fully present in your unique being is a gift to others and brings glory to the Most High.

Much of what we have been taught about ourselves and the characteristics of the Creator of the universe came from indoctrination. Traditions have become the foundation of our lives, and truth requires us to seek and to go deeper. Our thought process and the image we have of ourselves and life in general are tainted by society's version or are passed down. It is our responsibility to investigate.

I was once so defensive about the version of God and religion I grew up with that anything outside of those set of rules was false. I had a bias mindset, and renouncing the spirit of religion and asking for truth removed blinders I willfully wore.

I am grateful that a former pastor of a church I attended strongly encouraged me to pray for revelation on my own. In doing so, dependency on what the preacher said or other's definition of spirituality did not keep me so confined. It caused me to question, search for answers, study the Bible and history for myself, and weigh information.

I do not proclaim to have out-of-the-box thinking either. I am still seeking, learning, experiencing divine connections, and trusting Elohim with my path in life. I am still peeling off layers of truth. The last long-term relationship I had was fruitful as to knowledge and wisdom.

I know being connected with this person helped me spiritually elevate as he challenged me to acquire knowledge and pray for truth often. Second Timothy 3:7 says, "Ever learning, and never able to come to the knowledge of the truth." I spent years learning Bible stories and teaching and interpreting them to people, but I was blind to many truths I have come to know today.

One of the first truths I had to deal with was myself. Much of our energy is spend worrying about what others are doing when the biggest assignment is ourselves. Self-repair with the help and guidance of the Creator will take care of revolving issues.

We have been giving a set of statutes and commands to live by, and the key is to apply them. Most settle for being good or doing something that appears good when our goal should be to live righteous. We all get off the path sometimes, and prayer is one way to stay rooted.

CHAPTER 4

*Therefore I say unto you, what things soever you desire when ye pray
believe that ye receive them, and ye shall have them.*
> —*Mark 11:24 (Cepher Bible)*

A Miracle Prayer

As you know by now, some of my greatest prayer experiences were
spent by myself. I recall the afternoon that I was stranded in the
emergency room-restroom stall drenched in blood. From the waist
down, streams of red liquid slid down my thin long legs to the floor.

Puddles of it quickly formed. The cramps increased off and
on and were strong enough to force panting breaths and moaning.
While trying to get this blood flow under control, there were more
than a dozen people occupied in the emergency waiting room.

I yelled to the top of my lungs, "Someone come help me!"

Still, no one came. I cannot imagine the hospital walls were that
soundproof. No one could hear me, and I did not hear a peep from
anyone either. With my arms stretched on each side of the restroom
stall trying to hold myself up, the pain was so great that it buckled
my body forward almost to the point of falling down.

Spreading my legs and feeling the urge to push, out came a
blood clot as big as a one-pound bag of pinto beans accompanied
with warm liquid. In fear, I continued shouting for help. No one
responded. I guess no one even had to use the restroom. I was alone.
I took off my blouse worn to church that day to control the blood
flow, but the blouse was useless in seconds. It was soaked.

Suddenly, I thought about my cell phone in my purse that
was out of service. The cell phone service was cut off two days prior

due to nonpayment. Therefore, I did not bother to keep it charged. Somehow, I still thought to reach for it.

When I attempted to turn it on, nothing happened. The phone was completely dead. So there I was in a tragic moment praying. My 911 call was to the heavenly Father. I asked Him to help me. Although the actual dialect that day has faded, the outcome of the prayer request is sealed.

Ironically, about a year before this restroom experience in the emergency room, I worked in the telecommunications department of that same hospital. We were required to know the extensions of every department including the emergency room and triage nurse desk. With the cell phone clinched in my hand, I prayed continuously, "Father, send help."

My body was growing weak, and the small stall in the restroom started to look blurry as the feeling of dizziness came over me. Still praying and calling for help, there was an intense sense to press the power button on the cell phone.

Surprisingly, the phone lit up as if it was fully charged. At the same time, my body felt charged. I was shocked and in a state of temporary disbelief. I could not believe the phone came on. Words have no justice of what went through my mind in this moment.

I dialed a number using the extension to the triage nurse desk, but the first part of the phone number was wrong. Despite the misdial, the most grateful feeling came over me because the phone was working. It was a miracle! The pain started again, and the urge to push was strong. Out came another blood clot the size of the first one. To better describe its image, it looked like liver. More blood, more warm fluid followed.

Still holding tight to the cell phone, I glanced over at the phone to see if it was powered. It wasn't. I prayed. Another attempt to turn the phone on was successful. To my surprise, there was a dial tone. The first three numbers of the hospital finally registered in my mind. Dialing the complete number with restored memory of the seven-digit phone number, the nurse answered, "Truman Medical Center triage desk, may I help you?"

I rambled so fast that the nurse could not understand me.

She said, "Slow down. Where are you?"

Very slowly, I said, "I am in the women's restroom located in the emergency waiting room."

I did not know how long that phone would work, so in speed words, I told her that there was blood everywhere. Then the phone went completely dead. I tried a couple more times to turn the cell phone on, but it would not work anymore. My phone had no battery life, and there was no dial tone.

A few minutes passed, and three emergency room workers burst in the restroom with a rolling bed. Everything happened so fast that all I remember is one person talking to me a lot, one person cutting off my clothes, and another person putting those huge blood clots in a pink plastic pan.

I was placed on the rolling bed only wearing socks. As one of the workers reached for the door to open it and wheel me out, I squirmed on the bed, and through the pain, I grabbed hold of the white coat jacket and said, "I don't want to go out in front of these people naked."

The other worker rushed to get a sheet and came back to cover me up. The look on the people's faces sitting in the emergency room was priceless. They were amazed of what was before them—a young woman undergoing a rescue mission in the restroom of the same area they sat.

Now that I was beginning to feel safe, my thoughts were captured by the prayer that miraculously got the cell phone to work. I was in a trance. All I could think about was the supernatural effects of what happened.

The doctors and nurses presumed I was mentally checked out by the loss of fraternal twin babies. Instead, I was astonished by the act of supreme power. The pain, the restroom struggle, or the embarrassment of people finding out about my four-and-a-half-month pregnancy did not compare to this strong testimony of faith in Elohim.

I did not speak to a statue or call out to the universe. We serve a universal Creator, and I specifically called out on the all-powerful Creator of heaven in the name of His Son who responded.

Someone might assume that eventually, a person could have entered the restroom to find me just to discredit the hand of the Most High. I spent over forty minutes in that restroom alone, and no one showed up. A history of being anemic with the amount of blood loss I had is not a good combination either.

Prior to this episode, physicians counseled me about getting a blood transfusion for low blood levels. I never took it to heart and refused. The effects of prayer from this experience caused me to yearn for more of the Father. When people say that they don't believe the Almighty Elohim exists, I'm baffled. They have not called on Him and tried Him, or they have outright ignored Him.

Prayer manifests and proves His existence when met with faith. Faithlessness is next to godlessness. Self-reliance can never produce this kind of outcome. Elohim's acts and miraculous events are not new though. The Bible is filled with many stories and testimonies. Those Bible stories I heard all my life sounded like fables but eventually came alive in my personal life.

A lot of people claim to know the heavenly Father but do not believe Him to be omniscient. Confession of faith is not the same as knowing, hearing, and testifying of the one and only heavenly Creator. Spiritual decay and the rise of occult systems are becoming a way of life like in the days of Noe.

Reverting to prayer is a sense of emergency these days. The kingdoms that exist are in a battle for souls. Electing to pray is an urgent matter and a necessary decision not only for your personal life but also for this dispensation of time.

Elijah, a prophet of the Old Testament, is considered a man of prayer. He spent much time in solitude, but whenever he appeared on the scene, public demonstrations unveiled the power of Elohim. Elijah put his heart and soul in prayer in an age where people were growing disinterested in the truth of Elohim's Word.

On many occasions, the heavenly Father responded to Elijah's prayers to the point of stopping rain and the burning of an alter to vindicate Elohim's name. From his prayer, a widow and her son survived starvation. Elijah's prayers were full of power.

We can easily marvel at his prayer life in the book of 1 Kings. It went well beyond the credentials of the Most High for personal gain and personal experiences. His mission was to convict the conscience of people to convert their hearts fully to Elohim. Prayer performed in the right way and with the right intent brings results.

Praying with intensity for concentrated purposes takes attention and expectation that glorifies Elohim. I cannot be talked out of what happened to me the day I prayed and a miracle appeared. It was a stone of faith placed in my life forever.

CHAPTER 5

*Then ye shall call upon me, and ye shall go and pray
unto me, and I will hearken unto you.*
                              —Jeremiah 29:12 (Cepher Bible)

Prayer Is Not Religious

Prayer is not restricted to organized religion but is simply a dialogue with the heavenly Father. Anyone who has a life that consists of prayer is already aware of this. We should not be content with a prayer doctrine without personal experience. I went to one church all my childhood, and prayer appeared to be spooky, conditional, rehearsed, or for appointed occasions.

Growing up private prayer did not really resonate outside of seeing my mother pray alone. My family has a strong religious background. To give a glimpse of what I mean, my grandmother has been a member of the same church for over sixty-five years and my mother over fifty years at another church.

As a child, we would go to church at least four times a week through sun, rain, sleet, or snow. Church in the seventies and eighties was long programmed services, and there were strict rules to follow.

I can paint a picture of what strict was like. One Sunday as a small child, I left Sunday school heading toward the sanctuary where everyone met for the main service. A respected church mother grabbed me by the arm and bent down to me eye level. She was fussing about the sleeveless dress I was wearing.

Confused of why she was upset, I started whimpering. She told me to be quiet and twisted the skin on my upper arm. She pinched me so hard. On another occasion, I was slapped in the mouth with a twelve-inch wood ruler for having on earring studs in church. I started thinking that the God responsible for mean church folks was not for me.

If it wasn't that, it was the sermons and prayers about hell that scared me. As a child, sometimes, going to church felt like going to the haunted house. The church lighting was extremely dim, and the microphones were really loud. If there was any kind of prayer going on as a child, it was me praying fervently to stay out of hell. That was about the only personal prayer I remember.

My belief in Elohim and His Son was introduced at home and confirmed in church. Belief in Yahshua and accepting his redemptive power is the first step. After that, I always understood relationship with the heavenly Father as attending church. All those years spent at church did not teach me much about prayer though. Of course, people prayed in church because it was on the church program to do so.

At a prayer revival, I vividly remember how one of my brothers desired to get the Holy Spirit and to speak in tongues as evidence of receiving it. I believe to this day that he viewed it as a way to get superhuman powers to match what he read in comic books about superheroes. It's my guess and his own theory to tell.

Nevertheless, he was hit in the back (not in an abusive way) by one of those church mothers. After seeing this, I started thinking foaming at the mouth and saying, "Thank You, Jesus. Thank You, Jesus. Thank You, Jesus," as fast as I could were prayers that granted someone holy power and the gift of tongues. I am not trying to belittle the church or the sincerity they had at the time, but I must explain what prayer in church looked like to me as a child.

In most cases, going to church made me feel forgiven. It made me feel righteous and cleansed. I did my due diligence, so I was safe in my eyes. Attending church was a ritual my family expected, so I stayed with that pattern just about all my life.

To me, prayer at church or prayer at home together with family was considered having a prayer life. I prayed when I woke up, over my food, and before I went to bed. That was a lot of prayer activity to me back then, and since I carried through with it religiously, it was exceptional as far as I was concerned.

Thinking back to childhood, I remember the mornings my mother required me and my siblings to say this prayer when we woke up every morning:

Thank you Lord to let me live
To seeeeeee
Another day that I
Have never seen before.
Amen

After we were all fully dressed and ready to go, we all stood in a circle holding hands for prayer before we went to school. Collectively, we prayed this family prayer that hung on the front door:

We need one another
We love one another
We forgive one another
We work together
We play together
We worship together
Together we use God's word
Together we grow in Christ
Together we love all men
Together we serve our God
Together we hope for heaven
These are our hopes and ideals
Help us to attain them O God
Through Jesus Christ our Lord
Amen

Before each meal, we prayed this prayer in unison over our food:

God is good
God is great
Let us thank Him for our food
Amen

At night, my mother lined us up on our knees against the bed, and together, we said this bedtime prayer:

> Now I lay me down to sleep
> I pray the Lord my soul to keep
> If I should die before I wake
> I pray to God my soul to take
> Amen.

I know these are universal prayers, and we partook in it. I could not get these prayers out of my head even as a young adult. They were branded. I even passed down these same prayers to my children. Although the prayers were formalized, my mother's intent was to show us the way of connecting with Elohim, and for that, I am extremely grateful.

Moreover, we were eyewitnesses of my mother's personal prayer accounts too. My mother mostly prayed in private and periodically in the presence of her children. We did not always clearly hear what she was saying, but we knew that she was communicating alone with Elohim. At least, I identified prayer as essential in my mother's life.

According to Lauricella (2012), "Haplin (1984) similarly suggests that parents need to be attentive in their own prayer, for adults have the opportunity to grow in their relationship with God in order that they may be examples to their children." Most of her behavior and attitude toward prayer is fixed in my memory and has been a testimony in my life.

To this day, she has a strong private prayer life. She may have a religious nature, but her prayer life is not religious. After experiencing trials and triumphs in my adult life, it became clear that I did not have the prayer life my mother exemplified. I lacked a true connection with the heavenly Father, and I desired more.

As I grew older, I started understanding increasingly the importance of personal one-on-one prayer. As I came to know the heavenly Father for myself, my prayer life was revolutionized.

I learned that righteous prayers call for intervention, and there is a difference between learned prayers and supplications from the heart. Recited prayers can never replace authentic prayers. It's a start-up kit. As a child, the recited prayers were mostly said in a group setting. The problem with liturgical prayers is that it can be marked as vain repetition.

It may be okay for purposes of introducing prayer to children but should not become heartless lip service. Heathens were known to practice prayer rituals that eventually became meaningless, programmed, and almost robotic prayers. To have a flourishing relationship, there must be freedom of expression.

Next to the command to pray is an open door for intimacy with the heavenly Father that leads to willful obedience. I was looking for something deeper and wanted more than premade generational prayers.

CHAPTER 6

Let us therefore come boldly
unto the throne of grace
that we may obtain mercy and
find grace to help in time of need.
　　　　　—Hebrews 4:16 (Cepher Bible)

My Path to Personal Prayer

Incidents of prayer that contributed to my current prayer path is broad. There are episodes that come to the front of my mind instantly. In the beginning, I prayed a lot externally, and gradually, prayers became more inward. Prayer is constant today, and I've learned to manage when to pray outwardly and inwardly.

I chuckle within as I reminisce on the time I pulled up in my 1998 silver Grand Prix in front of my babysitter's house after work. As I opened the car door, a lady who looked to be early to midfifties was walking down the middle of the street with a liquor bottle encased in a brown paper bag. She was swearing and talking to herself, and the closer she got to my car, I felt the urge to pray.

This was around the time my faith had been restored and heightened. I joined a different ministry other than my childhood church at around thirty years old and committed myself to be a devoted member of this ministry. There was a zeal activated, and I felt invincible. As I stepped out of the car and the lady was approaching me, I felt impressed to say something. Before I knew it, I said, "God wants me to pray for you."

It immediately caught the lady's attention, and she was shaken out of her trance. As we moved out of the street, I repeated the statement: "God wants me to pray for you." The glass liquor bottle dropped to the ground as the lady lifted her hands up in total reception of what I said. The noise of the glass breaking caught the attention of a porch full of people nearby as I begin to pray for her. The lady started thanking the heavenly Father loud enough that everyone around could hear.

After the prayer, I started encouraging her to deal with the issues eating her up inside. Given the mindset I was in at the time, I probably encouraged her to ask Yahshua to come into her heart. I remember the lady receiving everything that was being said and confessing that she had been drinking for a long time and wanted to stop.

She mentioned something about headaches and asked me to pray for her in that area too. I may not recall every detail, but I cannot forget this day. As I was walking toward the babysitter's house, I was in disbelief about what just happened.

It felt natural to boldly proclaim this lady's deliverance, and during the prayer encounter, I did not care what was going on around me until afterward. I then felt weird and couldn't belief I just did that. I gave this strange lady my phone number and told her to call me if she wanted someone to pray with her.

I think back and find this hilarious mostly because of my level of boldness. This is one of many times I prayed at the drop of the hat with strangers. I still would do it today with a little more discretion.

Another thing I did on my prayer path was pray over the phone with people I knew. If it was not someone at the ministry I was attending, a friend, or a family member, it was 5:00 a.m. prayer on the phone with a group of wives who agreed to collectively pray for our husbands.

Some of the wives wrote out their prayers, and others prayed on the spot. I did both. We took turns praying for forty-five minutes to one hour daily for a couple of months here and there. Instead of griping sessions about our husbands, we agreed to do a group prayer on their behalf. A couple of us had serious issues going on, and we were trying to support one another in the best way we knew how. As things got out of hand, we knew prayer support would be the best solution.

Praying with others took precedence in my life at first. Besides, I could relate to it more from childhood. When our family gathered once a month for family meetings at Grandmother's home, we prayed together. It was the first item listed on our family agenda.

We even came up with a family mission statement to recite after prayer that we all looked forward to. It would not be unusual for a few of us to huddle before the family meeting to pray about a situation we did not want other family members to know about yet. They would grab me and my cousin Jojo and say, "Can y'all two pray for us about this situation?" Praying with someone else was familiar.

My private prayer life is what needed work, and I was starting to get used to it. Communing with Elohim in private is how I received instruction to write a letter to the family to come together as a unit more often. I wrote one letter, made copies, and mailed it to individual homes and set a date to start monthly meetings.

For fourteen years, our family met as a whole every third Sunday of the month. An average of twenty people met faithfully to fellowship, exchange business ideas, encourage entrepreneur and career advancement, plan family trips and gatherings, reward school-aged children, and more.

The family meetings were the one thing that kept us bonded. A generation of children was part of a functioning village until members of the core group relocated to other states. On special occasions when we meet today, there is always prayer. It's our foundation.

Our family definitely has a prayer culture that has been influential in my life; however, my personal prayer path was affected by personal events and experiences. There is a single event in my life that I know for sure progressed my prayer life and that was when my oldest son ran away from home. He was sixteen years old in 2007, and I was devastated.

I did not see it coming, and he did not show any signs of disturbance or trouble. Out of my four children, he was the quiet one and was always very mannerable. It is possible that I ignored the signs because I was so busy.

The responsibility of mothering my children surely was a big part of my life. So was working a full-time job, operating a part-time hair business, organizing family meetings and events, being devoted to many responsibilities in church, and everything else in between.

For five years of their school-aged years, I was a full-time college student and was helping my uncle and brother with their business ventures. So yeah, I probably did not recognize a slight change in my son's behavior. It could not have been too drastic, or else, it would have caught my attention.

My eldest son was an honor student all his scholastic years, and I did not have to convince him to work on his grades. He had never been suspended from school or had a fight to my knowledge. He was at the end of first semester of the eleventh grade when he ran off, and I did not lay eyes on him for five whole months.

He did not return to school. He did not call or step foot in the house. The affliction I had the first month he was gone was tormenting. I was in another world and speechless. Worried sick about his well-being, I continued doing everything I normally did and tried to take on more activities to numb my emotions. I knew that once I got home at night, it would all hit me, and I did not want to deal with it. It was too painful.

Well, I did not have a choice but to face what was happening, and I begin praying nonstop for my son. It was a couple of weeks after he was gone that someone spotted him walking with a friend. It was good to know that he was okay, but I did not know the reason why he ran away or what he was being exposed to.

As I prayed daily, so much was revealed to me, and I knew what to pray concerning him and his return home. I went from physical hurt in my heart, to grief, to constant weeping, to trusting Elohim totally. I started making declarations of faith until he came back.

My son returned home and graduated from high school on time, and our bond was stronger than ever before. Periodically even at thirty-two years old, he still apologizes about running away, and I tell him to not feel guilty or be ashamed because that event literally changed my prayer life and took it to another level.

More than that, I am grateful to be close to him and closer to Elohim who answered every single prayer request for his return home and everything afterward. This took me a layer deeper in prayer. None of what I experience was by chance.

As we walk our prayer path and results are experienced, there are a few characteristics about prayer to keep in mind. We must be sincere about our request while honoring the heavenly Father. This means we should actively listen to receive guidance. Prayer is not about doing all the talking. Whether morning, noon, night, or any other time, we should set time aside for prayer and not just in crises mode.

Daniel in the Bible is a great example of one who took his prayer time seriously. Not only did he make time for it, but also he did it in secret. Unlike the pagans who prayed to get the attention of others or convince their many gods to bless them, Daniel's alone-time praying was precious.

On this journey, I have discovered the value of praying alone in secret. The best thing about our Creator is, He knows what we need before we ask it; however, He delights when we meditate on Him during our prayer transactions. Our souls are satisfied. Our walk with Him is strengthened, and the inward acknowledgments of the heart help us to express His magnificence. As we become stewards of prayer, we are marks of those who are upright.

PART 2

THE PRAYERS OF OTHERS

—

CHAPTER 7

And if we know that he hears us,
whatsoever we ask, we know that we have
the petitions that we desired of him.
—1 John 5:15 (Cepher Bible)

Red's Prayer Request Granted

Everybody has a life story, but not everyone has a prayer story. My friend, Red, does, and over dinner at a Mexican restaurant, she is sharing how she prayed over a decade to have a child. I remember celebrating in joy when she found out the news; however, I did not know the extent of what she went through to conceive. As I am sitting across the table from her hunched over and dipping chips in queso-sauce appetizer, I was like, "Girl, you really prayed all that time?"

She said, "Yes, I believed God."

Red sounded solid about this experience. She went on to tell me how she had fertility treatments and minor surgeries off and on for seven of the ten years. Her doctor was concerned that an adhesion on one of her fallopian tubes was decreasing her chances of getting pregnant. As she was telling me this, I was eating faster and faster and engaged intently at the same time.

Red said, "I was even going to have an in vitro."

I said, "What is an in vitro?"

She said, "They were going to take my eggs and inject it with my husband's sperm."

I learned that she did not do it because after so many years of trying to get pregnant with the help of medical technology, it became too expensive and overbearing. Red had moments of being discouraged, and inferiority raised its head every now and then.

Nevertheless, she knew that if it could be done The Most High had the power to do it. Red mentioned how Abraham and Sarah gave birth to a child of promise at an old age. Without either of us elaborating, we both understood why she brought this up. Red was nearing forty years old and knew there could be adverse outcomes given her age.

After our entrees were served, I started flooding in questions, but Red wanted to keep pace with the sequential story and ignored my anxious energy. I calmed down my excitement of her reliance on prayer so she could finish her testimony the way she wanted to give it.

Red proceeded to say that she surrendered to what God could do and went on with her life without worrying about how it would happen. She prayed and made her request known as usual without giving up. During Red's years of waiting, she helped raise nieces and nephews and even became a foster parent. She greatly enjoyed it but still desired a child of her own.

I was like, "Didn't you get a prophecy about your pregnancy or something?"

Red said, "I was just about to tell you that next." She said, "One day, a family member told me they saw my mother's neighbor who lived across the street, and he said when you see Red, tell her to come see me because I have something I need to tell her."

Red decided to visit her neighbor's church as she did periodically. Her mom's neighbor was a pastor. During this particular visit, Mr. Johnson (or should I say Pastor Johnson) said that Red was going to give birth to a boy child. He also prayed for her, and she remembers the prayer staring something like this: "Father, you know her heart. You know what she wants."

Red fully received the prayer, and it confirmed what she had faith for all along.

Not long after, Red had a doctor's appointment to schedule a hysterectomy. Despite all the suggestions to permanently remove her womb due to complications with a fallopian tube, nothing stopped Red from believing what the Almighty could do.

Red said, "While I and my doctor were talking about scheduling the hysterectomy, I suddenly remembered what the pastor told me. I said, 'Dr. Garth, wait! I meant to tell you that a pastor told me I was going to have a boy child.'"

Dr. Garth was supportive of this and responded, "One thing I won't mess with is God's work."

This shifted the whole idea of performing any procedure, and the doctor said that they would revisit the conversation in two years to allow for conception.

Red continued to visit the church, and the pastor would ask her about the doctor's report about being pregnant. He was anticipating what the heavenly Father was going to do in Red's life. The report was the same, no baby yet. Of course, that did not stop Red from believing Elohim's report.

Pushing my plate back, I said, "Wow! How many years passed when the pastor was asking about the doctor's report?"

Red said, "The two years I and the doctor talked about were coming to a close, and that would have been around ten years, maybe a little more."

Then the day came when she and William went to Walgreens to fill his prescription. While they were waiting, he said, "I am going to buy something for you."

Red said, "What?"

William said, "This!"

"Is that a pregnancy kit?" she asked.

It was four days prior when Red was spotting off and on and her breasts were feeling full and painful. Nothing about pregnancy crossed her mind. Besides, she would not know what the symptoms were like anyway because she had never been pregnant. With kit in hand, Red and William hurried to her sister's house nearby whispering and huddling about a $100 bet about whether she was pregnant.

Red's sister blurted out, "Whatever y'all are whispering about, I want in on it."

Although Red was feeling certain she would win, especially since she was taking birth control pills to manage menstrual cramps, she lost the bet. The tinkle on the stick immediately turned the lines blue, which meant Red was with child. If there was an inner shout, Red was rejoicing.

At her first OB-GYN appointment, it was confirmed that Red was three weeks and four days pregnant according to the ultrasound. Nine months later, she gave birth to her son. This prayer story is one of faith and patience. I am sure there were times Red wanted to give up, but she knew with the Most High, all things were possible.

How many would have given up on this possibility weeks or months into praying? There are things in life we have to simply endure. Red waited over a decade. Her request seemed to be delayed, but it was not denied. Elohim is a giver of gifts and rewards the faithful.

Red's testimony reminds me of Hannah in the book of 1 Samuel. Details about how Red prayed are not referenced. However, we know for sure that she prayed and believed consistently to have a child. Elohim heard her request the first time but delivered on His word at an appointed moment. Hannah's prayers are vivid. She prayed in desperation. She wept, cried out, and pleaded for her barren situation to change.

On top of that, she was tormented by the insults from her adversary, Peninnah, who had a fruitful womb. Hannah's soul was in much sorrow. The best remedy to resolve her grief was prayer and divine connection. The honor of Hannah's character is patented by refuge she found in prayer. Not only did she cry out often, but also she worshipped in a nonritualistic way.

Hannah's soul was poured out through her sufferings. It was so internal and intense that it gave the impression of drunkenness. Her prayer fervency was a direct channel to the Creator without wishing ill on her harasser. It was Hannah's persistent petitioning in private sessions that established the position of womanhood she desired in society.

Hannah was frowned upon for a while. She was embarrassed by her condition, but in Elohim's timing, her relationship was evident through her granted request. She gave birth to a son and named him Samuel, which means "heard by Elohim." Samuel was destined as a highly devoted prophet and judge of Israel. Hannah's single act of frequent petitioning and waiting affected future generations.

Prayer stretches beyond our personal desires. As others see your life played out, they may inquire about the hope of your calling, and it gives you the opportunity to share the heavenly Father's interworking in our individual lives.

My friend Red and Hannah's prayer petitions to bear a child are centuries apart, yet the results are the same. They prayed, endured, and had faith even when it seemed impossible. One apparent difference was, Red had one child as requested and Hannah bore six children. Hope by the world's standard is not like praying and hoping in Elohim and all He has in store for us.

CHAPTER 8

Praying always with all prayer
and supplication in the Ruach [Spirit],
and watching thereunto with all
perseverance and supplication for all qodeshiym [saints].
—Ephesians 6:18 (Cepher Bible)

Mama's Interview about Prayer

Intrigued most of my life by my mother's devotion to prayer, I nestle on the sofa with one foot under my rear end and the other leg dangling off the sofa ready to hear details about Mom's prayer life. This is one person who lived a life of prayer before my very eyes. The stance she has in life against odds is remarkable and supernatural. She is the epitome of the phrase "if you are going to pray, don't worry, and if you are going to worry, don't pray."

While mom is sitting next to me in her grand presence of calmness on the sofa, I asked her to tell me about a memorable prayer experience as a child. She took a few minutes thinking about it, and to my surprise, she didn't remember much about prayer in childhood. Since I grew up in a family so devoted to church, I figured her memory of prayer would be a little different from mine, but it was not.

Mom remembers my grandmother mumbling a prayer sometimes, but nothing stands out beyond that. The most significant memory is the neighbor Ms. Robinson who was a boarder in the same home as Grandmother.

Even though she rented space in the living room of a two-bedroom bungalow and everyone shared the kitchen and dining room relocated to the basement, Ms. Robinson was still considered a neighbor and was responsible for introducing a dedicated church life to the entire household.

Grandmother attended the same church as Ms. Robinson with her three children until she branched off to a different church. Mom alternated going to church with them both, and the only thing she remembers is that prayer was long and boring.

In the early fifties, men mostly prayed and led church services, so she rarely saw women pray in the open. Saying a prayer under your breath seemed to be the way to go, and my grandmother still does that to this day. It's hard to tell if she is praying or talking to herself about something. Mom said that her prayer life did not really begin until later.

She started out journaling her feelings, and eventually, it evolved into prayers. This sounded all too familiar to me, so I must have followed her footsteps. Mom was married at the age of fifteen years old to my dad, and writing her concerns about husband and child was some small respect of prayer. She journaled feelings of regret for the path she was taking, and later journals were about getting spiritual assistance from the Almighty regarding dilemmas of being a young mother and wife.

Prayer became more profound around eighteen years old when Mom placed membership at the church she currently attends. She has been there now for fifty-two years. Mom is thinking back on the reverence people once had in church and the importance of a prayer life. To her, it was the testimonies of others at church who expressed the power of prayer.

I am sure that I was in these church settings but did not comprehend testimonies about answered prayer as a child. This brings me to reiterate introduction of rehearsed prayer to small children and explaining to them at some point to talk to Elohim as like they do a person. Mom told me that prayer became her lifeline as a young adult and continues today.

As Mom picks up on my deep interest of what she is saying, we agree to migrate to the dining room table so we can be face-to-face and continue with questioning and discovery. I entered the following dialogue to learn more about Mom's prayer life:

Me. Go back as far as you can, and describe a time you prayed earnestly about something and it came to past.

Mom. I went to a vocational school for training in the medical field at around twenty-two years old, and at the end of the state-funded program, I prayed for a good job so I can take care of my children. My prayer was answered, and I was hired at a well-known hospital. My prayer request was fulfilled at a time all odds were against me, but I knew I could depend on God.

Mom retired from her position in the medical field after thirty-eight years.

Me. Yeah, Mama, you know I am a witness of what it is like to pray and depend on the Most High.

Mom. I want to tell you about a few instances of prayer on the job that come to mind.

Me. Yes, please share.

Mom. There was a foreign employee from Nigeria who worked in environmental services. We spoke in passing as I and others did out of courtesy. One day as we greeted, our conversation extended to asking about how things are going at work. In the middle of small talk, the gentleman started complaining about stomach pain. He looked uneasy and was holding his stomach as he was telling me about it. I asked if I could pray for him, and he agreed. I thought it was a good idea to step on the side of the elevator out of the way so we could have a little more privacy and not make a scene. I asked if he believed in God, and he said, "Yes." I prayed and asked God to remove his pain and discomfort. Two weeks later, the gentleman saw me again and eagerly thanked me for praying for him that day. He said that there was no more stomach pain. He seemed very grateful for the prayer result.

ME. You do not say much in public. I never knew you did anything like this especially at the workplace.

I really had no idea Mom had the boldness to ask people (practically strangers) to pray for them. I am looking stunned right now. My thought of Mom being a quiet and behind-the-scenes prayer warrior just shifted. I've always known her to pray in private alone and with family or listing names in her prayer book, but she went beyond that. We continued our dialogue.

MOM. Another prayer instance is when a doctor who was a top-notch surgeon received prayer. I was transcribing his orders and noticed a sudden pattern of his patients dying, getting sick, or going back for more surgeries. Unlike the other doctors in his group, his patients were not doing well. He was starting to get frustrated about this each time. One day, the Holy Spirit told me to pray for that doctor. I felt hesitant at first but then asked to talk to him. I said, "Can you give me a minute to speak with you when you are available?" The doctor was busy and could not talk to me that day, but within that week, he made time. We went into the locker room for privacy, and I said, "I do not know if you believe this or not, but the Holy Spirit asked me to pray for you." I asked him if he believe in God, and he said, "Yes." I extended my hands so we can touch and agree in prayer. I prayed for him as the surgeon that his patients start getting well and that he would not lose any more patients. Prayer went forth about five minutes, and thankfully, no one else came in the locker room. The doctor gave me a hug and thanked me. Within the next few weeks when the doctor's surgeries started again, his patients were recovering better and were not falling off anymore. I do not know if it was a different technique he was doing or a change of pace when performing surgeries. All I know is the Holy Spirit said, "Pray for him." His frustration before was known, and he was popular for being one of the best surgeons in the hospital. It was a change and turnaround after that prayer. I could tell that the doctor had a different appreciation and admiration for me because of the prayer. He was always nice and pleasant anyway, and I am glad he allowed me to pray for him. He did not have a high-and-mighty attitude in his position.

Me. Wow! How interesting.

Mom. Other employees knew I kept a prayer list and would ask me to put them or someone they knew in the prayer book.

Me. I knew you kept a list of people to pray for like relatives and friends, but I was unaware you added people from work too.

Mom. Yeah, I not only focused on the list or prayed for people in person but also came to work in the mornings with my hand slightly lifted out and walked past each patient's room in my unit praying for their healing. There were twelve rooms on each side, and I did this for five minutes or so before clocking in.

Me. You mean to tell me that you have been in my life all this time and I did not know the depth of your prayer life? (*Mom chuckles while I am bucking my eyes.*)

Mom. People at church knew I worked in the hospital and would ask me to check on other members who were hospitalized where I worked. They may have been in another unit or on another floor. If so, I would go pray for them before or after work and sometimes during lunch breaks.

Me. I have so many more questions, but we will end here and resume on another day.

I concluded that Mom has a seasoned prayer life, and from childhood until now, it is threaded in every part of her life.

—

CHAPTER 9

Mama, Pray for Us Continually

Most of us know someone who is dedicated to prayer. My mother is one of those people, and I had to continue my quest of finding out about her prayer life. Her prayers for other people are continuous. I asked Mom about a time she prayed and felt closeness to Elohim that words could not describe. She said that when we were younger, she was walking to the bus stop feeling heavyhearted.

She said, "God, why did you allow me to have all these children?"

The heavenly Father's answer came in a matter of two seconds. In a sweet, still voice, the reply was, "To teach you how to pray." Mom said tears immediately started flowing. The answer gave her comfort and assurance. She talked about how praying helped her to mature and come out of shyness. It also helped her not to be so introverted.

With eight children and a host of grandchildren and great-grand-children, her prayers are nonstop. It would take another book to share some of those prayer stories. There are so many of us, and she literally has an individual relationship with us all. She is a confidant who does not unveil what is said to her. She listens, encourages, and prays about concerns of others.

Mom said, "It does not take long extravagant prayers to reach God. He has what you need, and He hears you." I then ask how her prayer life was affected when two of my siblings spent nearly thirty years in prison each. The question was unpredicted, and Mom

45

took a deep breath and sigh. I discerned that this was something that weighed on her still.

She said that she felt like a failure and felt as if she should have protected and talked to them more. In her private prayer time, she asked the heavenly Father things like, where did I fall short? What could I have done differently? Was I too anal about my life and not concentrating on theirs?

Mom stated that it was good to bring out her concerns to the one she knew would hear her and there was not always an immediate answer to prayers. "Sometimes, you just need Him to talk to," she said. What helped her out of her stupor of guilt is when she wrote one of my brothers in prison about how she was feeling as parent.

He wrote back and said, "Stop blaming yourself. You did not raise us like this. These are decisions we made. You were about integrity and showing us the right thing to do."

The ridicule she endured from one of the cases being high profile is something many probably could not withstand. She was questioned about her son's case at church and in the workplace, as well as by others who knew or heard about it on the news and in newspapers.

To get through this tough time of hurt, disappointment, and humiliation, she prayed. It gave her a sound mind, strength, and comfort that Elohim was with her. The response she gave to people, rather insensitive to her feelings or not, was, "I've given it all to God."

Mom said, "I know we all have shortcomings, and I am surely not a perfect parent."

I interrupted her and said, "In my opinion, you are perfect."

I said that because I have half the children she had and do not come close to what she offers to us and other people. In my eyes, she is a gem. I am glad my brother said what he said to her because it reduced mom's guilt that she internalized for years. "No one but God knew about my personal pity party," said Mom. She just asked the heavenly Father to help her with herself and how she was feeling.

When my two siblings were in prison all those years, Mom prayed for their protection, and they were protected the whole time. She prayed for their mindset and for them to learn from their mistakes. One of my brothers mentored many people while he was incarcerated.

When he was released, he later started a probation-and-parole service for ex-offenders to help them adapt to life outside of prison. Mom prayed that they would come home safely, and she continues to pray for the one son who remains in a facility.

My mother also shared how she prayed for her grandson, one of my brother's only son. During my brother's incarceration, she frequently visited her grandson. It came to a point where she did not know his whereabouts because he and his mother moved. She was concerned that he had not been around the family for five long years. She partnered in prayer with a friend for his return to the family.

Within three to four months of touching and agreeing in prayer, her grandson came walking down the street toward our family headquarters. It was my grandmother's home for nearly fifty years and the central meeting place for all family.

I am sharing this particular story because a few years after this reunion, my nephew was shot and killed. His murder remains a cold case to this day. It was the last year in high school, and he was months away from graduating as one of the top students in his senior class. He was gunned down walking home from the bus stop after studying at a public library and had a college application in his pocket.

The presumption was robbery, but to this day, no one really knows why he was targeted. It was the prayers of my mother that helped usher my nephew to spend the last few precious years with our family. This is only a fragment of the story my mother was eager to share.

Within a year of this incident, there was so much family tragedy, yet we were charged to pray in and out of season. Psalm 34:1 says, "I will bless Elohim at all times and his praise shall continually be in my mouth." I could go on and on with numerous prayer stories, and what I have shared is a tip of the iceberg.

I could add how Mom prayed for my sister who was prepped on the table for a late-term abortion. She was seven months pregnant. While my mother was praying for her to reverse her decision, my sister changed her mind about it. Her youngest son is now thirteen years old. Prayer increased discernment for Mom, and I know this is one way she was able to manage such a large household.

Mama's prayers are like a spiritual insurance policy for her children, grandchildren, and great-grandchildren, and some of us are following those footsteps. Our prayer journals could be prayer books. I love how Mom starts a new prayer list every month.

Whoever is born in any given month is automatically added to the prayer list. As people ask for prayer or if she detects someone is in need of prayer, they are added to her monthly prayer list too. Mama's prayers are about us but not secluded to us. It is circulated everywhere.

CHAPTER 10

Surely Adonai Yahuah [Lord God] will do nothing
but he reveals his secrets
unto his servants and prophets.
                    —Amos 3:7 (Cepher Bible)

Being a Prayer Vessel

Revelatory events and matters have come through a woman who stands four feet, eleven inches tall. She has overcome so many challenges and has a no-nonsense personality. She is caring, humble, and fearless in the spirit. She will tell anyone rather family, friend, foe, or stranger, "My name is Donna." She does not like to be identified by titles people call. Calling her by her first name is good enough. She despises being called a prophetess and only wants to be known as a vessel of God.

She grew up listening to people say their title with more importance than their given name. She told me how people are quick to announce their function or group belonging when a person's name and character should carry the weight.

"Titles and denominations do not reflect who you really are," she said.

She does not mind letting anyone know that titles are mostly man-made, and people hide behind them all the time. The kingdom of God and her service to Him are what matters most.

Ms. Donna is a praying woman and utilizes her prophetic gifts. Some people are afraid of the things she speaks and confirms about their life, and others are amazed. She said that her ministry started in high school. She saw things going on in a person's life and told them about it.

She is a firm believer that if someone speaks something about your life you do not already know or have brought before God yourself, then it is probably a false prophecy. In high school, she revealed things to people she would not have known on her own. She kept secrets of others and prayed for them.

She said, "I told my peers even at a young age to fall in love with God, and I still have the same message for everyone else today."

Sometimes, she is met with resistance when walking up to someone, but if given spiritual permission, she will look at a person square in the eyes and give them a divine word of encouragement, confirmation, or rebuke all in love. The heavenly Father uses her to minister to people as she goes. People from all walks of life can attest to the accuracy of her gift to reveal the Father's plan or warning for their life.

For example, I worked for the judicial system for more than eight years, and three years prior to resigning, she told me that she saw me working downtown at a law firm and there were two women attorneys—one on my right and one on my left. She described their hair color and personalities. I thought that this was absurd. I secretly thought, *Is she just coming up with stuff?*

I was comfortable in my role at the courthouse and had not planned to leave anytime soon. However, I entertained the idea of working at a law firm a couple times. Three years after this prophecy, I resigned from the courthouse to pursue a business venture. It took a year to realize the venture was premature.

Lo and behold, I landed a position at a law firm downtown. I'd forgotten all about what was said to me until months of being at the new job. I called Ms. Donna rambling with excitement about the prophecy she told me years prior. This shared memory does not touch the surface of things she has revealed.

This testimony is not to validate the behavior of religious fanatics who misuse their gifts to manipulate people, nor is it to promote magic, sorcery, or acts of dark spiritualism. I stand against such things but uphold how Elohim operates through people as He chooses. Those who study to show themselves approved are aware that most of what is written in the Bible is revelation.

Ms. Donna told me her spiritual abilities come from having a surrendered life to the Most High God and a life of constant prayer. What I love about her the most is, she lives a simple life and accepts whatever Elohim tells her to do. There is so much willingness even when she knows that sometimes, her obedience comes with suffering for a time to produce a righteous outcome.

I asked Ms. Donna to tell me about her prayer life, and this is what she shared: "Prayer time is around 4:45 a.m. everyday. It is a significant time. I pray for the nation, spouse, siblings, children, and others. I ask for direction for what the heavenly Father wants me to do. You got to talk to Him like you are talking to a human. He is there even though you can't see Him. Get to know him for your personal self. He will give you what you want and need."

I call Ms. Donna "Ma" for more than one reason but mainly because she is like a spiritual mother to me. *Ma* shared a testimony with me of why she started getting up at 4:45 a.m. over forty-five years ago. She prayed the whole time carrying her two sons asking the heavenly Father to help her with them. She explained how there was limited-to-no help while her children were growing up.

She had additional responsibilities of caring for her father and grandmother who raised her before their passing, as well as a sick brother. Her hands were full working two to three jobs at a time and caring for others. The only source she chose to rely on and the only one she could talk to was the heavenly Father.

Her relationship with Elohim was most important and was built over time through consistency. She remembers never praying for food. It was always provided without depending on government assistance. The one time later in life she received food coupons, she did not know what to do with them.

She tried to buy laundry detergent with it because it was so foreign to her. The point is, she relied on the Most High for everything. Ironically, someone would come along and fulfill her needs and desires, and she knew who put them up to it. *Ma* is certain about the difference between asking someone for something versus asking God.

She was so in tune with Elohim in prayer that even the death of her two sons was revealed to her ahead of time. I remember the day we sat at her kitchen table drinking coffee, and she told me how it was revealed to her that her younger son had about a year and a half to live.

She did not know the day, time, or hour, but the time frame was given. She was warned to prepare herself. Within the given time frame, her son passed away, and it was actually preparation for the death of her second son who passed away five years later around the same time of the year.

Through prayer, the revelation of these two events happened, and the promise was kept that they would be taken. Both of her sons passed away in their sleep. One was thirty-three years old, and the other one was forty years old. I am amazed of her resilience and how much stronger she is in her faith.

Today, she expands her arms around others and challenges them to trust Elohim for everything over the world's standards. *Ma* has been called upon to speak and encourage others and has given her testimony countless of times to prove we are overcomers. *Ma* believes that storms in life will come but will not last.

She finds safety and peace in the Most High God and gives all credit to the heavenly Father for her ability to stand after the loss of her sons. Charisma, popularity, or validation is not of interest to her. She operates with righteous motives and is yielded in obedience. Like anyone else, *Ma* has flaws and may miss the mark sometimes. She says, "We all fall short." Even a just man falls seven times and gets back up. In such moments, we must repent to be restored to right relationship with Elohim.

The assertion is that Elohim is in the center of her life. Revelation of hidden things is provided in so many instances of the Word.

The testimony of Donna is not one of doom and sadness. It is a reflection of Elohim's light shining on His servant in the earth realm. To this day, she gives more praise and honor to Elohim as supernatural peace is bestowed and transferred to others. Ms. Donna, who I call *Ma*, is guided through prayer and strengthened through prayer and credits it as the channel for her divine connection.

CHAPTER 11

*For the kingdom of Elohiym is
not meat and drink; but righteousness,
and peace, and joy in the Ruach Ha Kodesh (Holy Spirt).*
—Romans 14:17 (Cepher Bible)

A Praying Grandmother

Grandma Susie is ninety-three years old and has been one of the most active prayer warriors I have ever personally witnessed in my life. She is my paternal grandmother and has worked as a city missionary for about sixty years. It is spring 2022, and I dial her number so she can pray for my oldest brother over the speakerphone.

He was rushed to the hospital for excruciating stomach pain and upon arrival was in the operating room for emergency surgery after a few quick tests. When Grandma Susie prayed for him hours after the surgery, the room was illuminated. Her prayers have power and are effectual and fervent.

The three who were in my brother's hospital room felt electrified as she prayed with much energy for my brother's healing. My brother in a vulnerable position allowed us to see the tears rolling from his eyes as he laid flat on the hospital bed. You could see the peace come over his face at the sound of Grandma Susie's voice.

As Grandma Susie lay her prayers to rest, she said, "Jr, you are going to be all right. Give your life to God even more. Your voice sounds good, and I hear your strength. You are going to be okay."

This was a relief to hear because the doctors told my brother that if he had not come to the emergency room when he had, he would have died. I knew it would take the authority of Grandma's prayers to assure my brother he would be okay. Grandma releases prayers of faith without a faint heart or a feeble mindset. She is admired of this by our entire family and is a precious jewel especially because of her spiritual roots.

Growing up, I watched her wear a white dress, white stockings, and white shoes. This was her daily attire. She had white lined up in her closet always ready and willing for kingdom tasks at any place and at any time. She either drew or scattered a crowd once she started praying.

I remember one time she stepped on the scene in the middle of a house party in the late eighties. My brother Jr. was a known DJ in the city, and he threw house parties most weekends. This one was at our house when Mom had to work the graveyard shift. Just when the crowd started showing up around 8:00 p.m., Grandma Susie showed up.

We were not aware that she was in town. When she walked down the basement stairs where all the action was, she immediately started praying. Within five minutes, everyone was standing in a big circle holding hands. The party was over before it got started.

This was one time no one could sneak away. If they tried, she called them out and made them get back in the circle for prayer. Someone was always touched or reciting the sinner's prayer before she was finished, and someone was equally upset. That's just the way it was.

Grandma Susie has been called all kind of names from Holy Roller, super saint, crazy, overzealous, and many other names. Her life has been threatened multiple times, and absolutely nothing stopped her from working in the vineyard. At the age of thirty-three, she gave her life to the Most High and never looked back. She has so many accounts and testimonies of healing and deliverance, and I am excited to share some of them.

One time, I asked how she got saved, and she told me about a lady called Minister Trice who lived across the street from her that was responsible for her turnaround. Grandma said that she mocked Minister Trice, and she teased how she wore a choir robe and held weekly Thursday-night church service in her home.

She looked at her like a religious extremist and wasn't fond of her dogs. One Thursday night when the minister's service was out, she called Grandma over to have a word with her. Although grandma was hesitant, she proceeded to go across the street to see what Minister Trice wanted. Once they were face-to-face, Minister Trice said, "I had a vision about you. The Lord told me that He was going to send you to me."

In disgust, Grandma said, "For what? Is that all you wanted to tell me?"

Since Grandma was not receptive, Minister Trice just told her that God was going to send her and left it at that. That was the jest of the conversation, and Grandma hurried back across the street to her seven children.

What Minister Trice predicted came to past. Grandma Susie became extremely ill. She was a full-figured woman and became very frail from the illness to the point of almost not being recognized. The doctors told her that she would not live to see her seven children grow up because the illness would kill her.

For four days and four nights, she could not sleep, and the doctor prescribed her sleeping pills. During this illness as she laid in the bed, she said that God told her to arise from her bedside. He told her He would not take her life. He instructed her to go across the street to His servant's house and that she could help her.

Once she got to Minister Trice's house, she called an elder at the church to partner with her in prayer. Within thirty minutes, he arrived, and the two of them begin to tag team in prayer for Grandma.

The minister and elder prayed for Grandma's healing and for her to be saved and filled with the Holy Spirit at the same time. It was this encounter that turned Grandma Susie's life around the rest of her life. The woman she talked about was the same example she lived out. She has been a servant of the Most High all these years.

More than church and religion, Grandma Susie truly has a heart for souls. When she told me this testimony, she quoted Psalm 105:15, which says, "Touch not mine anointed, and do my prophets no harm." She said, "You can speak against God's servants, but you will not get away with it." Grandma referenced this because of how she spoke against Minister Trice and how people later spoke against her while she performed kingdom work.

Grandma Susie's fire for the Most High God has never went out. When called to duty, it only intensifies. Even at the age of ninety-three, she says, "I might have slowed down, but I won't stop." She told me how her church family gives her a strong reminder of her lifelong faithfulness and says, "It is okay to rest now." I told her I concur with them. They too have witnessed her evangelistic work for many years.

However, we all know that as long as blood is running warm in her body and there are souls to be reached, you will find her praying. Grandma even prays on a prayer line daily. There are times where she needs to call someone to pray for her too. She is not ashamed to admit that she is not exempt, but the prayer line is open for her to pray for others.

As I inquired about Grandma Susie's prayer and ministry testimonies, she provided unforgettable instances that I am going to share. One time, she and Minister Trice were coming from a church revival, and Grandma was under the anointing. She said that she was preaching on the way home. People who stood by were offended by her activity and threatened to throw scalding, hot water in her eyes.

They said that if she did not shut up, they would burn her eyes out. Some people intervened to keep violence at bay, and others called the police. When the police arrived, Minister Trice frantically told them how the bystanders threatened to cause Grandma harm. Through the whole ordeal, Grandma continued to pray out loud. She is never moved by how uncomfortable others feel when being utilized as Elohim's vessel.

Back then and even now, she is not ashamed of expressing the truth of Elohim's Word. If she discerns someone is in the need of prayer, nothing will stop her from praying for them. Since Grandma continued to pray aloud, commotion was stirred, and the police took her to jail for disturbing the peace.

Minister Trice pleaded to be taken to jail with Grandma even though the offense did not come from her. She did not want Grandma to be alone. Grandma repeatedly told Minister Trice to stand back, but she insisted to go with her to jail. It was not unusual for them to protect one another. One police finally said, "Well, let's put her in the wagon since she wants to go to jail so bad. There is room for her too."

When the two were booked in, the police took their Bibles and anointing oil from them. They were one cell away from each other and continued to pray. Both were released the next day and started shouting the victory right outside the police station, which could easily be another charge of disturbance.

Grandma's testimony reminds me of when Paul and Silas were on their mission in the book of Acts Chapter 16. They were seized by authorities and accused of bringing an uproar to the city after commanding a familiar spirit to exit a fortune-teller.

The masters of the fortune-teller complained and turned them in, and Paul and Silas were thrown in jail too. That did not stop them from singing and praying. A way of escape came for them and the other prisoners even to the point of one of the prison guards and his household being saved.

It is amazing how similarities in kingdom work are consistent throughout time. It witnesses the heavenly Father's character of winning people to do His service so others can be saved, be delivered, be set free, and enter into eternal life. The message of the kingdom relates to the Messiah's rule in heaven and earth, which can flow through His subjects.

We are to seek the kingdom and invite Elohim's kingdom to reign in our daily lives. It does not consist of man-made rules and regulations. It is of righteousness. So many from the ancient text were beaten and jailed and became outcasts because of their obedience and life in Elohim. This still applies today whether through public shaming or a single incident.

Grandma Susie understands this concept and therefore has not been controlled by the opinion of others or societal confinements. Though much of our family have experienced moments of embarrassment like with the house party mentioned earlier, we respect her love for Yahshua and His mark of righteousness on her.

CHAPTER 12

And the prayer of faith shall save the sick,
and Yahuah shall raise him up
and if he have committed sins
they shall be forgiven him.
>   —James 5:15 (Cepher Bible)

Grandmother Called to a Great Work

Grandma tells me of a one-day mission where she only wore the dress on her back with a Bible in hand, three handkerchiefs, and a couple bottles of oil in her purse. She was heading to her hometown in Osceola, Arkansas, from St. Louis, Missouri, in the early sixties.

Draped in all-white clothing, she was riding the Greyhound bus without anyone knowing she was coming or going. Even her close sister was not supposed to know she was in town. Grandma said that this is the instruction she was given by God, so she did just that.

Her feet landed her in an open place in the town. She was declaring the word and praying for people in the street. A bystander called the police because people gathering around her to listen was blocking traffic. She was faced with another instance of disturbing the peace.

Grandma told me, "Girl, don't you know a colored police asked me if St. Louis was a big-enough place to preach and pray in?"

He asked Grandma why she came all the way to Osceola to do this. Grandma's mindset was obedience to Elohim's instruction. Ultimately, Grandma completed her assignment as given to her and got back on the last Greyhound bus leaving the town.

Four to five hours later, she was back in St. Louis well into the night hours. It was late, and she decided to take the shortcut home walking from the Greyhound bus station when a man in hiding was waiting for her to get closer to physically attack her. He had a knife in his hand, but thankfully, a police car was posted nearby watching the whole thing play out.

As grandma got closer to the man, the police shined the bright lights from their car on him to bring the attempted attack to a halt. The man ran off, and the police escorted Grandma all the way home and afterward warned her to not walk that path at night again. She repeatedly thanked them and knew the heavenly Father was the reason for this protection.

Grandma knew she was not in the best neighborhood. This was the same area she said the dope man came to hit her in the head with a pipe. He was tired of her talking about being saved and praying for people in public. Plus, she was interrupting a group of guys gambling on the sidewalk.

When she came toward them speaking and praying at the same time, the guys ran off picking up dirt with the dice along with the money they had on the ground. One man begged the dope man not to hit her in the head. She boldly told him, "Do what you gotta do because I am going to do what I came to do."

I said, "Grandma, did he hit you?"

She said, "No, baby, I was protected."

Prayer was so engraved in Grandma that she was sometimes sent home from work. When her children were younger, she cleaned homes for a living. There were no mops for her to use on the job, so she cleaned the floors with a rag on her hands and knees. The workers rode the city bus to Mr. Willman's office, and the workers were transported to and from homes for domestic work.

Grandma would get on the city bus praying for people and telling them to repent and be saved. She often quoted the scripture in Mark 8:36: "For what shall it profit a man, if he shall gain the whole world, and lose his own soul."

If she got to Mr. Willman's office still praying and carrying on, he would tell her, "You need to go home and preach or go find a church to preach and pray in." Then he would firmly say, "No work for you today." Grandma knew the risk of doing this, but it did not stop her.

She did her due diligence in and outside of the home, in and out of town, and everywhere she went. Grandma told me that sometimes, she gave a universal message to groups of people rather than praying for one person at a time. People did not accept what she was saying all the time. If this happened, she would declare a blessing and leave.

Grandma said, "You can't push nothing on people. Jesus said, 'Whosoever will, let him come.'" There were many times people fully embraced what she was saying. Grandma was often requested to pray for people who willfully accepted her message delivery. She frequently prayed in prisons, hospitals, and homes.

At the hospital she went to once a week, she prayed for people, fed them, or helped anyway she could. She was not paid to do this but was moved in her heart to be present for those in need. The hospital chaplains at one point confronted her and said that they were hearing rumors of her getting results. They said, "We are here every day and do not get these results." Eventually, they shadowed Grandma to see how she performed and tag teamed with her.

The chaplains changed how they approached prayer with the patients and their families to her method. They watched one time when a patient told my grandma that she was hungry but could not feed herself. Grandma sat beside the patient's bed and said, "Well, honey, we want your belly to be full and satisfied before we do anything."

Grandma took her time feeding the patient, and the Chaplin asked, "What should happen next?" Grandma told them to give the patient a word, and then she would pray. The chaplains who once sat in the office sitting around drinking coffee waiting to get a call to serve changed their whole routine of making rounds to each floor just as Grandma Susie did.

This was Grandma's routine at adult hospitals; however, she was given a vision by the heavenly Father to volunteer at the children's hospital too. She was told that she outperformed the hired certified nurse's assistants. It was never competition to her, only ministry. She bathed the children, dressed them, combed their hair, fed them, and of course prayed for them.

During Grandma's street mission and ministry, people gave their testimony of times she prayed and there was deliverance. One day, she was in her white praying near Forest Park in St. Louis, Missouri, and a lady ran up to her to say that she was cancer-free. Grandma did not recognize the woman, but the lady said that grandma prayed for her while she was in the hospital.

She said that Grandma asked God to heal her from the illness. The lady said that she had been praying to see Grandma again so she could tell her she was healed. Grandma said, "I'm sorry. It was probably someone else wearing white."

The lady said, "No! It was you who prayed. I prayed many days to see you."

A similar instance happened when Grandma did not recognize someone she prayed for. Because she prayed for many people, I am sure it is almost impossible to remember everyone. Grandma tells me about a homeless man she prayed for waddling on the ground. She asked him, "What happened to you?"

The man replied, "I was an educated man and once a schoolteacher." He told Grandma how he lost his job, his wife and two children, and his home after running with the wrong crowd. She remembered this after this same man spotted her in the grocery store and approached her.

He told Grandma how she prayed while he was waddling like a hog. He would go home after being on the street for days. He was dirty and smelly, and his wife and children did not accept him. After he received prayer from Grandma, that encounter led him to go to Goodwill to get a pair of clothes and shoes.

He turned his life around, went back home, and was restored to his family. He knew Grandma was of the Pentecostal faith and told her that he was attending a Baptist church with his wife.

Grandma said, "It only matters that you have given your life to God." She continued, "Don't worry about the denomination because only the pure in heart will see God."

After sharing a few of her testimonies, Grandma ended our conversation with a nugget to live by and to tell others.

She said, "Your mouth can say anything. What counts is what is in the heart."

She said a church member told her that COVID-19 came and everybody needs the heavenly Father. People are asking for prayer left and right. The song she sings after this statement is true to this day:

> It's gone come a time everybody is gonna need
>   the Lord
> God is speaking to the heart of His people
> You better pray while you gotta chance
> It's gone come a time everybody is gonna need
>   the Lord

Chapter 13

Trust in El-Yahuah with all your heart
and lean not unto your own understanding.
In all your ways acknowledge him
and He shall direct your path.
—Proverbs 3:5 (Cepher Bible)

My Prayer Perspective

I hope the prayer experiences shared so far were a little entertaining and provided a peek inside the prayer life of me and others. I have come to some conclusions about prayer and want to give an individual perspective. In my opinion, the idea of prayer and its function have been abused and misconceived. The way prayer is viewed and utilized should be reexamined and better understood.

Although we are all expected to exercise our right to pray, it is ineffective if not accompanied with the right motives and intent and it goes beyond doctrinal beliefs. Misappropriation of prayer and lack of understanding of its purpose leave so many in a state of defeat. It should not be loosely handled, nor should it be viewed only as a religious tool. Prayer is a necessity of life. To dismiss or ignore prayer all together can be damning and destructive.

I can't express enough that prayer is a way to interact with the Creator. Bible personalities are used as examples of approaching prayer in an intimate manner. The blunt of their stories reveals how they obtained guidance about many situations individually and on behalf of others. The God of Abraham, Isaac, and Jacob was their prayer source, and they yielded themselves to His power and instruction.

Frequently praying about the affairs of life was done with reverence. They did not just kneel, cry out, rant, or babble words and then go about their business. There is nothing new under the sun. Many of the concerns we have now are like the ones our biblical ancestors faced. Prayer worked throughout history, and it still works.

Further, we must realize that prayers can be rehearsed by anyone. The question is, who you are praying to and what is the origin of the prayer? Is it a ritual? What is the history behind the prayer practice? What makes it righteous? Prayer is communication but to who?

I've entertained looking into prayer cultures and discovered that my experiences praying to the Creator of the universe were similar to prayer experiences other cultures described. The difference is the root of the request, the purity of the heart, and the source. I cannot leave out the result. More than experiencing answers to prayers is power from the Creator we pray to.

The Bible is crystal clear that ancient people prayed to all kinds of gods and idols. There was always a difference from prayer to Elohim and other gods. The effects of prayer to Elohim, God of the Israelites, caused kings to convert and order the land to trust the God of the Hebrews. Nothing has changed as it relates to prayer and different gods.

Some people believe that they are wholeheartedly praying to the Most High without realizing they are praying to false gods. Others purposely pray to other gods, and surprisingly, they too get results that later prove to be a counterfeit. You must have knowledge of the Word to discern counterfeit prayers.

Let me share some of the things I found out about other prayer cultures. As we know, archaeologists study human history and activity and excavate sites. It has been said that world archaeologists have discovered stored prayers from old Greek and Roman ruins found throughout ancient Mediterranean. These prayers are better known as curse tablets.

In the tablets, the names of gods are invoked. Punishment is described. A victim is named, and an explanation of why someone incurred wrath is explained. The Bible instructs us to bless and curse not. We are to pray for our enemies and use warfare prayers as the battle. There were not any tablets discovered that related to blessing enemies, only cursed prayers. Therefore, I emphasize prayer to the Creator of the universe. Through Him, we invoke righteous prayers.

I was watching a documentary on television one day and saw people in Venezuela praying. There were shrine guardians on an altar in which the people prayed prayers of protection. Parts of the country were in ruins, and a cult of Holy Thugs who reached out to the dead was gaining popularity. The deceased thugs were worshiped as idols and were praised for stealing from wealthy people to feed and serve the poor when they were living.

One of the gangsters they worshiped was from the 1960s. They believed if they offered cigars, there would be answers to their questions. The scary part is that the cult of Holy Thugs held services remarkably similar to a traditional church service.

According to Adalbert G. Hamman (2020), "An adherent of tribal religion is aware of his dependency both in relation to his tribe and to the supreme being. He often addresses his prayers, however to various numina (spiritual powers); the dead, the divinities of nature, protective gods or actor gods."

Another interesting thing I found out was there are praytheists. This is someone who does not believe any god exists but enjoys the social or community aspect of prayer. Did you know satanists pray? Even religious extremists and cults pray to other gods knowingly and unknowingly. This is why the Bible warns us to test the spirits by the Spirit to see if they are of Elohim. Many people are entertaining familiar spirits unaware.

When praying, we must trust Elohim to perform according to His statutes and commands and not according to our own authority or religious cults and practices. Modern society is under the delusion that prayer is a quick fix solution to issues, and many have started to doubt, mock the idea of prayer, disbelieve altogether, or revert to strange prayer rituals. It's tragic!

Elohim gives outcome to prayer that is unmatched by anything else. We must know He works righteousness and produces victory. We must give him room to work in us, through us, and for us.

The prayers of the righteous profit the soul, guard nations, remove burdens, restore relationships, heal infirmities, serve as assurance in times of trouble, and more. Prayer to the right source, in the right mindset and spirit, avails much.

CHAPTER 14

Yahuah is nigh unto all them
that call upon him,
to all who call on him in truth.
　　　　　—Psalm 145:19 (Cepher Bible)

Prayer in Its Rightful Place

What is meant by prayer in its rightful place? In the grand scheme of things, a person is an extension of the kingdom in which they are associated. In Elohim's righteous kingdom are principles that will benefit your entire existence. When praying in faith, change is evident, and the fruit of the spirit will generate faith, love, joy, peace, forgiveness, and redemption.

The heavenly Father will hear your smallest to greatest concern. His presence and intervention are inarguable, and the only thing that will keep someone from knowing this is unbelief or someone with a reprobate mindset.

Prayers should be intentional with pure motives to get an active response to petitions. Emotionalism, logic, philosophy, or man-made doctrines are sometimes the cause of spiritual stagnation or unanswered prayers. Asking and receiving in prayer should not be taboo but purposeful so Elohim receives all the glory and honor for His work.

In the past seven years, my life was remodeled after praying for the spirit of truth and renouncing the spirit of religion. Since I was a child, I have always known some form of prayer, but it developed into a personal relationship as life progressed.

I do not have all the answers, and I am still growing. I was led to share my individual experiences that will hopefully uplift someone else. Prayer in its proper place will move you to seek the kingdom of Elohim and His righteousness and will unveil your path of life.

Like I once did, people rely on others to pray for them rather than praying for themselves. Although there is significance when others pray on your behalf, we should personally become acquainted with Elohim ourselves. After all, you are responsible for your life, and relinquishing it to others for repair is irresponsible.

Do not get me wrong. We do need prayer support from other people, but ultimately, Elohim wants to hear from you about your own life. If you truly desire change, thinking you are not good enough to pray is a flawed mindset. This mentality could make you a target for spiritual manipulation.

Now I am skeptical about who say they are praying for me because I'm unsure of who someone is praying to. It's not paranoia. It is awareness especially with the uprise of witchcraft, sorcery, and Luciferian doctrines.

One of the goals of this book project is to place importance on a private prayer life. Philosophy and teachings of today's church leaders graze over the significance of personal prayer. More emphasis is placed on prayer meetings, prayer vigils, prayer lines, and prayer requests among fellow believers or direct appeal to a spiritual leader.

These avenues may serve a universal purpose but do not lay a solid foundation for the masses to rely on a personal prayer life. Prayer is often too generalized or passed off to someone else. All you have to do is take a poll of people you know and ask them about their private prayer life. I promise you will be amazed at the amount of people who say they believe in prayer but do not have a prayer life. It is time to increase prayer activity.

In most cases, people simply do not know how to pray or understand the nature of the prayer exchange. We should model what Yahshua did in Matthew 6:5 and pray alone. There may not be a physical door to shut, but the point is to be in a secluded place.

He removed Himself from crowds and His inner circle to commune by Himself. Scripture does not paint a picture of Yahshua in a circle of prayer or as part of prayer groups. It was not forbidden; however, He prayed privately, taught the proper way to pray, and displayed a lifestyle of prayer. We must follow his example.

Like with any relationship, it takes frequent conversation to get to know someone. In a prayer dialogue, there is an exchange of talking and listening. You must be genuine and cannot approach prayer like it is a chore.

A person can pray all day or at designated times of the day, but if it is not with pure intentions or according to the Heavenly Father's kingdom's standard, it is probably a ritualistic prayer to any god or entity. You can say all the right words, but if your heart is far from Elohim and your motives laced with selfishness, you pray amiss.

It is our responsibility to pray daily on a personal level to evolve spiritually. Without prayer, immorality easily sets in. We become evasive, disconnected, and then ashamed to engage in prayer altogether. If you have ever been given the impression that you are not adequate enough to pray for yourself, that is inaccurate.

I learned this by yielding myself to Him in the rawest form. Nothing should make you feel unworthy to talk to Elohim. If you seek Him for help and answers, it will lead to repentance, restoration, right relationship and will produce life-changing results.

Over time, prayer was my safe place. It is a hidden world where I receive instruction on how to maneuver in everyday life. I am not perfect. For years, my life was a complete mess. I am flawed and still turn on prayer to work through shortcomings. At one point, I thought I had it all figured out, and I found out that my way of doing things was wrong.

Drawn away by lust and the cares of this world, I made horrible self-destructive choices that pushed me toward prayer. I was one of those people who painted how my life should go and prayed for the Most High to arrange things according to my own life plan. When trying to direct your own path, it becomes a fight of your will against the will of Elohim.

Being preoccupied and consumed with things going on in my life. I just couldn't seem to get around to prayer, nor did I make time for it. Sometimes, I was so busy doing good that I failed to do what was right or required. Eventually, I entered into submission. I'm loaded with situations that commenced me to pray and can never expose all of it. It's endless!

After a while, prayer time elevated to thoughts and conscience. I grew to depend on it. It became a way of life. When I am not in thoughtful prayer, I am setting a time to pray or give homage to Elohim in prayer journals. I have so many written letters to Elohim. My favorite time of the day fully devoted to Elohim is in the mornings. The more I understand the purpose and benefits of prayer, the more I do it.

We know it is right to pray, but the motivation to do it is not always about resolving issues. Prayer constructs and reconstructs lives, but it should also be filled with adoration and a grateful heart. When prayer is interwoven in every aspect of our lives, we tap into the inner instinct to praise. Our eternal being makes a connection, and Elohim's guidance is known and felt.

Comprehensive prayer

Heavenly Father, I come before You asking for forgiveness of my sins, iniquities, trespasses, and transgressions. Forgive me for the sin of the desires of this world, having doubt, being disobedient and for taking part in the lust of the eye, lust of the flesh, and pride of life. I ask to be delivered from fear, hate, gossip, idolatry, sexual impurities, and all forms of perversion and evil.

Heavenly Father, please remove self-righteousness, self-centeredness, self-criticalness, pity, strife, unbelief, uncleanness, unforgiveness, perfectionism far from me. Keep me from addictions of any kind, and help me to remove murmuring and complaining far from my lips. Father, please rid me of rebellion, resentment, and unsubmissiveness.

Your word in Matthew 16:19 says that You will give me the keys of the kingdom of heaven; whatsoever is bound on earth will be bound in heaven, and whatsoever is loosed on earth will be loosed in heaven. Therefore, I bind all evil, lying, unclean, tormenting, demonic spirts, and strongmen in the name of Yahshua HaMashiach, and I lose them where the Messiah sends them.

Cover me and cleanse me of all unfruitful works and vanities of this world. I pray that this request is granted according to John 16:23, which says, "Whatsoever I ask in your name you will give it."

I am thankful for this day and come boldly to the throne of grace to ask for protection, healing, deliverance, sanctification, redemption, and justification. I pray for cleansing inside and out and ask that You make me over so all things are new. Heavenly Father, I thank You for so many things.

Thank You for life, Your Word, Your mercy, Your grace, Your ministering angels, and Your salvation. Thank You for Your righteousness imparted, the inward voice, the inward witness, and all You created.

Sanctify me daily, and grant peace that surpasses all understanding. When trouble or hardships come, I pray that evil will not prevail. Thank You for Your provision. Thank You for being a wonderful counselor, the way, the truth, and the life.

Heavenly Father above, help me to be a doer of Your Word and to walk after the Spirit so I will not fulfill the lust of the flesh. Thank You that You did not give me the spirit of fear but of power, love, and sound mind. I pray to hear Your voice for my loved ones and that I am not deceived in any area.

Please set a clear path for us to follow. Let the word of my mouth and medication of my heart be acceptable and be of understanding. Let my speech be with grace, seasoned with salt, that I will know how to answer every person. Help me to abstain from all appearances of evil. Heal me and everyone I pray for from diseases, and redeem us from destruction, snares, and traps.

Remove all dependency of the flesh and oppression brought on by worldly systems. I pray that Your kingdom will be the sustaining power for life. Thank You for the kingdom benefits, which includes soundness of mind, kingdom authority, fruits of the spirit (love, joy, peace, patience, kindness, generosity, faithfulness, gentleness, and self-control).

Thank You for the impartation of wisdom, knowledge, and instruction as attention is given to truth. Show me how to be helpful in Your kingdom and how to serve Your divine purpose on earth.

So be it. It is done.

The End

References

Baesler, E. 2012. "An Introduction to Prayer Research in Communication: Functions, Contexts, and Possibilities." *Journal of Communication and Religion*, vol. 35, no. 3 (Fall 2012): 202–208.

Lauricella, S. 2012. "The Lifetime of Prayer: A Review of Literature on Prayer Throughout the Life Course." *Journal of Communication and Religion*, vol. 35, no. 3 (Fall 2012) 209–236.

About the Author

For over two decades, Arlinda McGee has faithfully served as a spiritual influencer in her hometown, Kansas City, Missouri. Whether in a local church, in small group setting, or through individual connections, she is known for transparency when sharing her personal experiences to inspire others.

Her goal is to encourage others to trust the universal Creator with their lives, to stand through trials, to become whole, and to overcome the causes of spiritual stagnation. She is marked by her resilience, which comes from having a consistent prayer life.

Self-discovery and spiritual growth are ongoing attributes as she avails herself to remain a student of biblical text. Ms. McGee is passionate about sharing kingdom knowledge while interjecting personal challenges she faces on her journey of truth to anyone willing to hear.

www.ingramcontent.com/pod-product-compliance
Lightning Source LLC
Chambersburg PA
CBHW021128130726
47988CB00003B/1203